WINDOW PAINS

Bruce F. Mase, Ph.D.

WINDOW PAINS

ISBN 0-89536-270-8
PRINTED IN U.S.A.

TO MY OWN CBS NETWORK
AND
ITS LOVELY EXECUTIVE PRODUCER

A BOOK

A cover
Behind which
Is
A page
Behind which
Is
A person
Behind which
Is
A mind
Behind which
Is
A heart
Behind which
Is
A soul
In which
Is
God.

ACKNOWLEDGEMENTS

Parts of any book are predictable. Part of me detests being predictable. Another part of me is glad that I am. Therefore, I will accede to convention and be properly grateful.

Acknowledgements present dilemma, the dilemma of where to tap into and where to stop the flow of a grateful, artesian heart:

* To my mother and father who found something warm to do on a chilly September evening in 1929;

* To the publisher, who enabled this manuscript to stop collecting dust on my shelf and start collecting dust on yours;

* To Donna Kauffman, who was born upside down, who thinks inside out, "experiences" everything, and who not so gently tells me when I am full of postpartum prunes;

* To William A.P. Bell, the mellow Scot, who is a dear Christian friend and my father-in-residence;

* To Duane Ruck whose beautiful photography graces these pages;

* To all my brothers and sisters of humankind who have helped to "fill the cup;"

* Finally and foremost, to the One who . . .

FOREWORD

The contents of this volume represent the thoughts, inspirations, and musings of a man well-acquainted with the commands of his Lord, and the human frailties that result in falling short. He writes from the stance of one who has experienced the emotional intensity available to us with other human beings; joy and fulfillment as well as grief and betrayal. The tone of the volume is set by the author's identification with the pain of change as he has experienced it, and as he has seen others struggle, resist, perhaps embrace that change which is constant in Christ. It is clear there have been visions necessarily given up and yearnings that have fallen on barren rather then fertile soil.

The author asks the question that all of us who pursue care-taking professions come to at one point or another — to whom does the shepherd go for holding? There is a certain solitary sense that is familiar to the individual who has chosen to be a care-taker. Often this is a position which by its very nature allows only a stance of certainty, of confidence, of strength, of self-sufficiency. One's own tears are often shed only in the presence of a watchful Spirit, and there are few indeed to whom the shepherd turns for holding.

There is no question, however, upon completing these pages that the author carries a profound faith that he is accepted, and that he moves in the forgiving love of Jesus Christ. There is also no doubt, despite an impatience resembling the disciples', that the author has experienced the frustration and fulfillment of loving relationships, however perfect or imperfect. We are indeed shaped by those who love us and those who refuse to love us. The window pains that have opened to fields of growth and chasms of darkness have also opened to allow fresh vision and a welcome light.

As a fellow care-taker and this shepherd's long-time friend, I know this work to be the author's personal contribution to harvest in a field where he has labored long. Surely because of it, laborers will increase and God's love will become clearer, even if through the pain of new windows.

Louine A. Vaughan

Ms. Vaughan is a psychotherapist in private practice in Denver, Colorado.

FACE

Many books have a preface. I have never quite understood this. When I see one, my logic becomes lustful. It thinks: Preface, Face, Postface. I cannot remember seeing a postface in a book. I have seen many, but not in books. After sermons, speeches, pastoral calls, bored meetings, and therapy sessions . . . boy, have I seen them. But I like to feel that I have only one face; many facets, I hope, but one face. Therefore, I will make a face at you.

Windows are for seeing. They are for insight and outsight. It helps if the glass is clear and undistorted. Insight and outsight can result in emotional and spiritual growth. All growth is painful. It means change. Change can make us dreadfully uncomfortable. Because of the content and intent of this book, it seemed proper to entitle this volume "Window Pains."

I seem to be irrepressibly hooked on two phenomena. The first is the aphorism. No, you don't have to look it up in your Funk and Wagnals. Definition has arrived. The following is from **The Random House Dictionary of the English Language,** which was given to me by a tactful Ladies' Aid group who felt I used too much slang in my sermons: "a terse saying embodying a general truth." I am quite sure that my love affair with the aphorism is a reaction-formation to the vice of verbosity, the preacher's peculiar brand of postnasal frippery.

The second is poetry. I thought I couldn't write poetry. Then one day I found that I could and immediately fell in love . . . again! This was one of the many collateral benefits of therapy. When I took my own "archeological expedition back among dead men's bones," a real solid block was uncovered in this area. When I was a little lump of clay being molded by many bony fingers, it seems that I tasted the tyranny of a towering inferno. That tyranny took the form of a teacher. A description may prove useful. She dressed in used drapes which hung in long, festooning folds. These were "gathered at the bodice," as they say, by a

naval brooch, a rather obscene cameo as I remember. She
was one huge wrinkle. In addition, she wore rubber
stockings, black brogans, ate onion sandwiches for lunch, and
smoked Muriels in the custodian's toilet.

Our assignment was to write a poem. It was an age when
I was discovering the divine mysteries of reward and pun-
ishment. I was eager to please, so I diligently set to the
task. The following day she called on me to recite before the
entire class. Joy of joys! Embryonic feelings of a future
Robert Frost boiled within. I dramatically delivered. Even
more dramatically she roared: "You call that poetry? That's
terrible. You'll never be able to write poetry." I was
trounced to tears and rushed to hide in my inkwell. Tragedy
of tragedies! For more than twenty-five years I believed her.

I can write poetry. So can you. Notice, I have not said
good poetry. As a poem, in conversation, remarked to me
the other day: "Why do you call me good? No one is
good but God alone." Poetry happens. Art happens. It is
the poets and the artists who then go about collecting a
conceited consensus to declare it good or bad.

With regard to the organization of the book, you might
call it an anthology. You might, but I won't. That sounds
like the "study of anths." Who knows, maybe it is. However,
I prefer to call it a collection, like you would collect stamps,
garbage, eggs, campaign buttons, service plaques, autographs,
mosquito bites, cross and crown pins, and so forth. Besides,
it sounds more religious. The first part of the book contains
a group of aphorisms. Some stand or fall alone. To others
I have added comment in an attempt to reveal how the train
got to the station. These are for reflecting. The second part
has a group of poems on various themes, in various moods.
These are for experiencing.

Why this book when today there is a plethora of such
from which to choose? There are two reasons. First it is my
hope that the aphorisms will stimulate your thought, thereby
being of value in your life and profession. I hope they will
act as a springboard from which to dive deeply into the pool
of your own person and discover the rich, buried treasure
therein.

Second, it is my hope that the poetry will encourage you to write your own. At least, I hope it brings you joy, new revelation, renewed appreciation, and that it will bless your spirit . . . as it has blessed mine to write it. I welcome your comments. Write to me in care of the publisher. If it seems desirable to share other writings, I know my wife will be pleased. She has had to clean around boxes of the stuff for years. Shalom!

Bruce F. Mase
Lima, Ohio

To many
It's offensive . . .
To think
Christ is the core
Even of the
Bad apple!
To a few
This is very
Consoling.

*Two men went up into the temple to pray . . . So many
I have met over the years see themselves as righteous rather
than as redeemed. The former position acknowledges no
sinful condition. Therefore, forgiveness is a meaningless and
irrelevant concept! The fact of this is demonstrated by
attitude and behavior. The resurrection is seen as a deserved
affirmation of an already accepted perfection. The concept
of God is stern judge who is "making a list, checking it
twice . . . " The latter position acknowledges a sinful
condition. Forgiveness and grace are meaningful and relevant
concepts. This fact is demonstrated by attitude and behavior.
The resurrection is seen as an overwhelming, inexpressible
gift, totally undeserved; a miracle that on reflection fills
the eyes with tears and wells the heart to overflowing
thanksgiving. The concept of God is loving Creator who
desires our return from self-imposed exile, estrangement,
and alienation.
Have you ever noticed that those who seem to revel
in the doctrine of election and other biblical dichotomies
seldom entertain the possibility that they might be among
the non-elect?*

Have you ever tried to find
The author in
Authority?

*What I accept as authority in life is quite revealing. How
I react to that authority is also revealing. There is a paradox
here. The more disguised and hidden I try to be about
"authorities" in my life and my feelings about them, the more
I reveal myself. It does not take long to discover a person's
"authorities," especially his ultimate authority. In time altars
become readily apparent, idols become readily obvious.*

*But finding the author is quite another matter. "Who
says so" becomes a rich arena for self-discovery. The
popular delusion is, of course, that "I do." It can be
shattering to discover that I am a speaker connected to an
amplifier attached to a turntable, on which is playing a
record I did not select. It can be very relieving also.*

There is a compensating wisdom
Born of the soul's deep anguish
But only claimed by the
Seekers of life's deeper meanings.

*****

The sparring is jarring . . .
Even to a champion!

*****

I asked for a fish
I was given a stone

*****

Pity the man
Who hails the nails
That impale upon the tree!

*****

Is it queer to fear veneer? . . . I must
Escape this rape of all my senses.
I find it worse to have a purse
Filled with sad pretenses.

A young woman called:
    Distress
    Urgency
    Anguish.
Someone laid a trip on her:
    Sanctification
    Is hair
    In a bun
    And
    No makeup.
And our Lord wept . . . again!

We are great reductionists. It matters not that such reduction is often artificial. We wrap it, box it, crate it, fence it, press it, chop it, and can it. Anything, just so we can "get a handle on it." We must be the master of mystery; idolatry in the form of the great god all-knowing. We reduce faith to a belief system, douse it liberally with dicta and dogma, and attempt to club people into submission . . . in the name of his love. Judge, jury, and executioner.

We may miss the point, but by heaven we can recite it by the numbers. "God is not mocked" . . . "He looks upon the heart." Only arrogant man can take the "pearl of great price" and reduce it to such paucity: a paucity of impious rules and regulations that masquerade as faith. The Lord desires a legion of lovers, not a wedge of wardens and watchdogs.

O Lord . . .
Keep me from using
Four-letter words.
The only ones worth
Repeating
Are felt by those who really
Know me!

Who cares for:
  Shepherds keeping watch
    Over their flocks
      By Night?

In the midst of merchandising and census-taking, in the midst of crowded motels and clogged inns, it often seems that no one except the shepherds is interested in the real events of the stable. And they have made the trip so many times before. They are very, very tired: lonely in a crowd, sad in a moment of joy, restless in the revelry. But then, who cares for the shepherds?

In the army of indifference there is direction: "Take it to the chaplain!" And where does the chaplain take it? The Great Shepherd loves. Underneath are his everlasting arms. Still shepherds need arms around them. Why cannot shepherds care for shepherds?

Well, Harry:
Your rage
Brought you
Center stage
No longer
On view
To only
A few!
Is it scary?

*****

The timid bluff . . . the bold bark.

*****

What is the matter with matter?
The matter with matter is
It matters too much!

*****

I just heard
A sweet voice on the radio
Telling of a sugar shortage —
Little does she know!

*****

A sneer so dear
He was
Reluctant
To part with it!

Most people fear further emotional debt
once they have had a note called.

Some people have high counterdependency needs. This means that for them to feel a sense of worth they must have others dependent upon them. They seek their opposite, that is, those who have a diffused sense of identity, a low sense of worth and self esteem. The latter become the liquid plastic to the former's mold. Such a relationship is very destructive and is destined to end in rejection. The over-dependency becomes a burden, the person attempts to move away, there is desperate clinging, and finally rejection resulting in deep hurt.

The overly dependent person is left with an even greater need to be close; however, now is added a deep fear of being close, a fear of being absorbed. A wariness sets in. The person begins to "look for the hook." Lifespace shrinks and living becomes even more unfulfilling. It becomes very difficult to "play it straight" when life is perceived as nothing but angles and curves.

It used to be
    That
        False faces
            Were worn only
                  On Halloween
How times have changed!

*****

Now I lay me down
To weep!
For I cannot sleep
With the feeling of
Betrayal!

*****

"Wasting" ourselves is sometimes
an attempt to disguise our feelings
of worthlessness. It helps to
preserve the delusion that there is
something worth wasting!

*****

A material serial
        is always
                "continued next week,"

A perilous brink
        avoided
                "in the nick of time,"

But whose end
        is known
                "in the beginning."

The marginal
Man
Walks the edges
Of life
Peering in . . .
Longing for
Gum drops!

Fantasy is one of this world's greatest seductions.
Fantasies are created for us daily. We laugh and say we do
not hear, we do not pay attention. Yet subtle is the erosive
force of constant bombardment. Even with the best radar,
some of the planes get through. Soon we are believing that
we can have the best of both worlds. With a foot planted
in each, the diametric movement causes a rending which
forces decision. We choose the soft, the easy, the joyless,
the hysterical, the barbaric. In windless drift, the chasm
widens. Now, vague outline only. Now a sad remembering,
for the cost, however high, compares not with the present
price. Yearning. Soon the man has his shoes nailed securely
to the floor. He can step out and move. But he hesitates
to do so because the shoes are so comfortable, so nicely
broken in.

Pressed

I am depressed by . . .
  lies expressed,
    love suppressed,
      evil impressed,
        good oppressed,
          the genuine repressed.

*****

I sometimes hate the weight of fate!

*****

A subrepticious serpent crawls the land.

*****

Tomorrow will bring something new:
Hertz "Rent-a-Friend."

*****

Why this valued vacuum . . .
  This dis-ease of emptiness?
I have come afoul of fear,
  The illusion of being full!

Could be
The marginal man
Trips on the perimeters
Of paradise
Because
He lacks the courage
To discover the
Diamond
In his own
Carbon dust!

*"The kingdom of God is within you." I will not quarrel
if you interpret the pronoun in the collective sense, meaning
the household of faith, the church, rather than in the very
personal, individual sense. From my vantage point, it seems
in many places, and with many people, the gospel is hitting
a stone wall. Preaching the "good news," that God loves
us and that Christ died for us, is not penetrating. Many
are suffering from such a diminished sense of self esteem
that they cannot hear, embrace, and accept that God loves
them, however much they may yearn to do so. This increasing
futility and emptiness causes these people to act out in
overcompensating ways which does violence to their deeper
values. This results in reinforcing and increasing the feelings
of worthlessness. To the person who despises and rejects
himself, it is difficult to hear that the kingdom of God is
within.*

*So emerges marginal man. Perhaps you know one. But
concerned Christians, how shall we lovingly touch this needy,
often desperate person? How shall we assist another to
discover that he is one of God's own diamonds? By making
him feel that he is good for nothing but to be "thrown out
and trodden under foot by men"? How did you become the
diamond you are?*

CHRIST . . .
      He is
      Lord of all
      Or
      Lord of nothing
This is a true dualism.

*****

        The peripheral saint
        May be the heart
        Of Christ . . .

*****

To drink
From a bitter cup
And still love . . .
To be baptized with
Dark waters of hardship
And still follow . . .
      The way of him!

*****

      I must zipper up
      My heart
      Against
      The cold wind of indifference.

What is the crime of time?

Time is a fascinating subject. It is a philosopher's field day. Pull down from your shelf any book of quotations. Under "time" you will be rewarded with a lifetime supply of quotes, even if you take two at every meal. The sages of the ages will tell you about time! But can anyone tell you about time? You can crowd it. You can vacate it. You can compress it. You can expand it. You can, can't you?

Time. Can it be stolen? Is it the thief? Is it the tyrant? Are you the fief?

I went to tear off his mask . . .
And to my horror,
I discovered it was his face!

*****

Tremendous vibrations
Are not necessarily
Beautiful music
Together!

*****

Hear!
Is it sound profound
That gives me such a start?
Dear!
Tis the groan of stone
Within a concrete heart!

*****

There are fluid
Mechanics
And mechanical
Fluids!

*****

True love . . .
The only
Soul food!

It is moving to be moving;
Cling to your rock,
Watch the clock!

Growth is movement. I find it very moving. Exciting adventure. It means expanding the emotions, the spirit to its richest capacity. Not everyone feels this way. The life process is dynamic. Some seek to make it static. They cling to their rocks and furtively peer at the clock. Time passes . . . ever so quickly. They truly need a piece of the Rock. But they have no free hand to reach out and accept it. They are clinging for dear life to their pet rocks. Fearful children, not growing up, simply growing older.

Is
The impetus
The power
Or
The power
The impetus?

Does a moment lean
   Upon another moment?
Or does it stand
   Alone . . .

*****

From the beginning
My Father
Was called to account
For the time
Spent
In his
Mother's
Womb.

I wish
My father
Could
Have kicked
His boot
Through the
Picture window!

*****

Today I discovered
The graveyard . . .
Of gentle hearts.

Little man . . .
Parade your power,
Cuddle your control!
You have bought
Life
At a very dear
Price!

Life style —
   . . . to burrow a furrow between
      the adversities of life!

"I have come that you might have life, and have it abundantly." There are those who look out at life and become frightened. They see it fraught with fatal hazards. They make a dreadful decision. Their "spirits" go underground. They tunnel through life, like moles who never see the sunlight. In the end they are successful if they have managed to survive and to avoid life's major catastrophies. Now what? Is life really some kind of sentence to be served? What have they received from the cross except splinters?

Divorce is on the rise—
This assumes marriage!
Not so!
Just that masks have met
Pretending
Intimacy!

To bask in the banalities
Of life
Is to commit
          Sewercide!

*****

Man cannot stand
The power of tenderness.
It makes him a sieve
To give!

Come death . . .
Complete
The burning of
My lonely years.

*****

Tis far better
To
Savor the moment
Than
To do obeisance
In
The temple of
Time!

*****

Ink is to a
Pen . . . as
Feeling is to
Reason!
Without their substance both are hollow; neither flow;
And to make their mark, they leave a scratch!

I passed by
Until I learned
To hear a tear
And
To see a cry!

*What is the sound of "one hand clapping"? What is the
sound of one tear falling? When I see a tear . . . when I
hear a cry . . . I may stop, out of curiosity, duty, superiority,
and I may say, "Hush your heart and dry your eye; it will
be better tomorrow." I may stop . . . and still pass by!*

How is a man measured?
Height?
Breadth?
Depth?
Core!

*****

Man can endure almost anything . . .
Except the threat of exposure!

*****

Do you suffer from hardening of the hearteries?

*****

My anger has a severe hold on me . . .
Or is it the other way around?

*****

Am I numb to some . . .
Or
Numb to all?

What does an end run really look like?

The allusion is not to football and "student body-right." It has to do with behavior. Example: If we feel that our needs and wants are not legitimate, or if we are blocked in filling these needs and wants directly, there is a great possibility that we will try to get them filled indirectly. This usually calls for some manner of disguise; it may call for an attempt to circumvent the "block;" it may call for an attempt to manipulate the person or situation to one side; or it may call for an attempt to exact from the person or situation a particular prescribed response. Such maneuvers do not satisfy because the deeper self knows the behavior and does not hold it in high regard. What does your end run look like?

Why the fear of falling? Perhaps it is reinforced
by the delusion of having gained great heights.
Remember, for the snake a fall is just a roll.

*Culture puts a high premium on achievement. Therefore,
I achieve. As in most things, the distortion, thus the danger,
is to be found in exaggeration. I can place such a value on this
that I may feel I am accepted not for who I am but only for
what I do. So instead of being, I constantly must be doing.,
The logical conclusion of this behavior is perpetual motion . . .
and a restless discontent. Lurking in the shadow is the fear
of failure. Failure: something which our educational system
does not teach us to handle creatively. In every endeavor, no
matter how small and insignificant, I can feel on trial. Life
can become a continuous "test" that I am forced to pass.
Under such pressure, ethics can become relative and the end
can justify the means, as we have dramatically seen in recent
years. And what of the joy of living? What happens to it?
Achievers are believers. The question is, in what?*

Today is
Hard.
I hope
To be
On
The soft side
Of
Tomorrow!

*****

When I hurt . . .
The pain smothers
Every pore . . .
Is this how it is
With you?

*****

Left in the lurch?
Search!

*****

Integrity means wholeness!

*****

I love a fire
In a fireplace
It affirms me to see
A log doing its thing.
Can we say as much
About ourselves?

Level is not necessarily even

*The dictionary treats these two concepts as synonomous.
I do not believe this is so in the human equation. Level
is not necessarily smooth. Even can be on a slant. Somewhat
like a piano, the emotional keyboard has eighty-eight keys.
The greatest goal of some people is to go through life
playing "chopsticks."*

*Levels of understanding can be very uneven. For example.
In our culture the popular "myth," promoted by most, is
that life has a spiritual base. This is one level. Evidence of
this concept's mythical quality is that we behave as if life
has an economic base. This is level two. The profound
reality is that life does indeed have a spiritual base. This is
level three. Thus the original postulate, promoted as a
reality in which we do not believe, is in fact real.*

It is a struggle to juggle accounts. Debits
and credits lead to a columnar view of life;
then comes rank and file.

Credit: *an entry of payment or value received on an
account.*
Debit: *a recording or an entry of debt in an account.*
Debt: *something that is owed; an obligation or the
condition of being under such obligation.*
Column: *a vertical arrangement, a row or list.*
Rank: *a number of persons forming a separate class in
a social hierarchy; a class in any scale of
comparisons.*
File: *a line of persons or things arranged one behind
another.*

*Pecking order . . . Then the mother of the sons of Zebedee
said to Jesus . . . Categories become concrete, perhaps because
we do not believe the great debt has been canceled . . .
"How's your wife? Compared to what?" . . . Pigeonholes
are for pigeons . . . ledgers do not live . . . the kingdom
beyond caste.*

Is it experience
Or
Encoded software
Of
Manufactured moments?

*Man is a machine . . . a magnificent, complicated machine.
He is metronomic movement, programmed mechanics, rote
response. Until he realizes that he is a machine, he cannot
cease to be one. Man spends his life asleep or awake. When
he is asleep, is he unconscious? When he is awake, is he
conscious? Are there different levels of being conscious?
Is conscious, self-determined behavior different from
automatic action?*

*Look again at what the New Testament says about being
asleep. Look again at what Jesus says about being awake,
the "he who has ears, let him hear" kind of consciousness.
The religious computer of his day was programmed. So
what's different today, two thousand years later?*

My thoughts are just
    Passing through —
Like a marquee
    In motion.

*****

Pollution:

Why care
If
The air
Be fair?
Tis the scowl
That makes
It foul!

*****

Do I wonder as I wander . . . or . . .
    Do I wander as I wonder?

*****

Do the pure obscure?

*****

Life is found in the daring and the sharing,
The universal caring.

I saw a mother kidnap her daughter and hold
Her for ransom for fifty years; the child
Paid the price in daily installments.

*The need for love and affection is universal. When I am
not receiving it, particularly from significant others, I can
become emotionally deprived. In such a state I am vulner-
able. I may adopt a wide range of self-defeating behaviors
in a bid to get this need met. I may succumb to panic and
fear. It is in this condition that the threat of the withdrawal
of love and affection can become a powerful tool for
manipulation.*

*We are told that love is not jealous, that it is not possessive,
that it does not insist upon its own way. We are told that
love does not treat a person as a thing. What, then, is this
entity in our culture that is masquerading as "love"?*

46

Despair crept in to lay hold upon the
    Web whose fibers were so tough . . .
T'was then I knew I had believed
    Just not quite big enough!

*****

                    The water-table of my tears
                    Grows higher as I walk
                    Through the misery of
                    Our land . . .

*****

Life
For some
Is a series of
Walter Mitty musings.

*****

            The church:
                That costly cathedral
                Where the answers go to die
            Because
                The questions couldn't belong!

Pleasing can be unpleasant!

Feelings of non-acceptance are very unpleasant. I feel that I am not accepted for who I am. I will correct this. I will become who I am not. I will become who "others" need me to be. Look! Look how hard I'm trying. Strange, I still feel that I'm not accepted for who I am. Feelings of non-acceptance are very unpleasant. Who is rejecting me?

Christianity: splinters of the cross!

*****

Which is more difficult:
   To curse God and die . . . or
   To curse God and live?
Which is more dangerous?

*****

A Savior's Birthday

Resignation
To
Indignation!

*****

O God:
Keep me hidden from myself;
For I am too much
For me to bear!

We have canonized
The Organization!
We kneel in awe to
St. System . . . the Golden-Mouthed!

*How strange: Some who would deny there is soul, much
less that they have one, often complain quite bitterly of
having "sold my soul to the company store."*

*For awhile in man's evolution, it seemed that he might
finally escape the pagan ritual of human sacrifice on the
altar of some angry god. But alas, he insists on remaining
quite primitive, refusing to understand that the angry idol
without is but a projection of the angry idol within.*

*Choosing to believe the myth of his own helplessness, he
continues to oil the joints of the machine that he himself
creates. In this, the tyranny of his own fear, he finds only
despair.*

Where do I belong?
I feel like a
Marble
On a billiard table!

*****

PAIN . . .

I try to tell you how
I truly feel —
The faint flicker in your
Eyes — fleeting in its
Presence — tells me how you
Long to hear what I say.
But you cannot, it is too costly.
I know, I understand:
It makes me very, very
Sad.

*****

I met the king-sized filters
Of your ears,
I see the mist-invested veils
Of your eyes,
I perceive the pasty, pastel drapes
Drawn securely
Across the windows of your heart:
And this makes us both
Uncomfortable!

In our unholy arrogance
We attempt to sell the sod
Right out from under God!

"This is my Father's world, and to my listening ears: All
nature sings and round me rings, the music of the spheres."
The ecological tree of life: A branch of biology concerned
with organisms and their environment; a branch of sociology
concerned with the interdependence of people, institutions,
and space. Man collects real estate. It is a good long-term
investment. He scrapes it, paves it, stacks it with blocks. In
so doing he hopes to purchase a parcel of belonging. Choosing
to forget he is but a transient guest, he continues to leave
behind a history of hysteria.

Paradox

I complain of pain
Though plain it's the main
Object of my life!

*****

CHURCHIANITY . . .

Is my name Abacus
That you should
Count on me?

This time not a cross:
Our Lord
Is
Clubbed to death!

*****

O GOD . . .

Pull back the curtains
Of my life
Lest they become
Shrouds.

The discovery of your purpose
Is your life's pilgrimage;
Once found, you are dead.
The secret is not to die
Before your time!

*If a Christian sees conversion as terminal . . . then it is.
This is one of the greatest mistakes in understanding the
faith. Conversion is the beginning of an exciting and joyous
adventure. Where it will lead only the good Lord knows.
What fun to read a book whose end you do not know,
whose last page you cannot read. But something puzzles
me. I know people who are avid mystery fans who want
nothing to do with the greatest mystery of all. Instead,
they write their own ending to a book that has no beginning.*

Born again?
How absurd!
Whoever heard
Of returning
From whence we came?
But then —
From whence did we come?

*****

Sermon on the Mount: Prints of Peace.

*****

Given a second chance
We kill him . . .
Again!

*****

Sometimes I long
To be wrong
In things that really matter!
This uptight right
Becomes a burden.

*****

Is the integer
Really found in
Fractions?
Is our integrity
Really found in
Fractures?
Lord, did you mean for us
To live
Only in the cracks of life?

Oh God —
What if the wall
Should fall?

*****

And fear
Weaved its wretched web
About this miracle
That is called
My heart . . .

*****

Human Dilemma

We can manage the Manger,
    We can corrupt the Cross!
But we can not . . .
    Retract the Resurrection!

O LORD . . .
                    The sinews of
                    My soul are
                    Sore.

I don't know about you, but my soul seems to have sinews. And they get sore. My preliminary diagnosis of this recurring malady is that it results from observing and participating in too many arthritic relationships. At the end of my day, as I sit before the fireplace (my closet has one) and take a much needed inventory, I am ever amazed at what I have collected. I sometimes feel like a magnet with iron filings. The sorting process is bittersweet, now painful, now relieving. I constantly marvel at the Master, how he handled what he saw and felt. Even with the spirit aflame, the soul can become inflamed . . . with too much pain and hurt. When this happened to Jesus he retired to the lonely place where "no one else can go," there to be soothed and healed by the Father's grace. When the sinews of the soul are sore, it is there I too must go, to the lonely place where "no one else can go," save the One who is already there.

Words
Cannot
Animate
Unless
From
The soul
They
Emanate!

Salesmen and preachers seem to know this. This knowledge may be intuitive or learned. But members of these two groups often conveniently forget this truth. They fall prey to the errors of misrepresenting their product or being detached from it. Salesmen and preachers must deeply believe in what they're doing. Without this deep, personal conviction they may make a "sale," but they will never "bring life" to another person. Depending upon their individual desires and motives, they may elicit a response from another, as a dead frog leg responds to a simple electric charge. However, with the removal of that temporary charge, the leg returns to its static state. There are many with a "Mary Hartman" mentality who can be so excited . . . temporarily. And their number in the decade of the seventies seems to be increasing. Beyond questioning the morality and the integrity of such emotional manipulation, which I do, I question the permanence of such response in terms of the kingdom of God. Raising the dead takes great faith, a ton of love, unlimited patience, and much hard work!

Many relationships today suffer from
Over-revolvement!

*****

They also serve . . .
   Who only sit and stare!

*****

It is hard to be a
Solid
In a fluid and
Hold your own!

*****

Would you borrow
My sorrow?
Or would you
Feel what is real?

*****

Why do we avoid each other's eyes?
Is it fear we will see something
Or
Is it fear we will see nothing?

I see: little boys trying to be men, and little girls
    crying to be held;
I see: little boys huddled together still pitching
    pennies at cracks in the sidewalk and
    little girls all dressed up trying to tame
    the tug of time.

*****

What hurt so cruel
To make a man
A tool of darkness?

Man is reluctant
To relinquish
His defense
Of pretense!

*****

The fair care,
They dare share.
Only the lonely
Play
The fame game!

Such a man lives in a world
Which dares to have no corners.

OH?

I believe that this is the world's shortest poem. It is entitled "Indifference." It's an old poem. It is as old as Adam's apple or as Eve's headache. With just the right inflection it can be truly representative of every person's most ignoble aspiration: to replace the remaining vestige of inconvenient feeling with the smooth whir and soft hum of electronic man, where every movement is a calculation and every conversation is a printout. It is a poem I have seen and heard recited by congregants, marriage mates, "lovers," parents, doctors, lawyers, and politicians. In a world of increasing dis-ease we have found the optimum protection, the way to be truly antiseptic and sterile.

GOLGOTHA . . .

Will
What
Happened
At
The skull
Ever
Reach
The
Heart?

I have always felt that the site of the crucifixion is some-what unfortunate. For many, what happened at the skull remains at the skull. Well-adjusted man needs psychological defenses. However, he gets in trouble sometimes in having too many, and in selecting very costly combinations. Walls have two primary functions: they keep out; they also lock in! A very common defense is the defense of intellectuali-zation. The feelings are "walled" off to protect against hurt and pain. People and events are encountered with the head. Practiced long enough, a person will eventually "think he feels," instead of feeling.

One of the greatest barriers to faith is this defense of intellectualization. In my head I can work out a reasonably acceptable series of beliefs and be miles away from faith. Chances are in the process I by-pass the volition. If so, nothing changes. Therefore, I can think I have faith and behave as though I don't.

POETRY

Is it . . .
   Rhyme sublime
   Or
   Taught thought?
Who is to say!

O Lord:
What can
Take the ache
Away . . .
Reaching out
To touch the
Final form,
The basal substance
Of the creature
You have fashioned
By the breath of
Nostril flare . . .
Realizing only
The fog that
Hovers o'er the bog
Of human misery
Mired in the mud
Of the
Monstrously mundane . . .
A benumbed nobility!
Are we a
New savage
With
The wheel?
Is our destiny
To traverse
The heavens
On tails of
Liquid fire,
Eyes too transfixed
On dials
To notice
The miracle
Unfolding?

You come to us,
We drive you
Away
With our
Abstractions . . .
And distractions.
You bid us
Come to you . . .
And suddenly
Cataracts at our
Core!
Now Lord,
Tis finally time
To zipper up the
Universe,
To fold in zenith
And the nadir;
For we have
Taken your
Great university
And fashioned us
A sandbox filled
With pales
And
Saccharin shovels!

Petition:

On the brink of living,
Twenty years of preparation for life
And then — and then,
Doors open, or close —
No one knows.
A full life is before —
To be used —
Where? How?
I'm ready, God,
Holding my breath,
Here I am,
Show me now.

I
Sing of the king
Nobody wants:
For his throne
In this world
Is filled with
Pretenders.
I
Sing of the king
Nobody wants:
For his throne
In this world
Is filled with the
Hiss and kiss
Of gardens.
I
Sing of the king
Nobody wants:
For his throne
In this world
Is filled with the
Spears and nails
Of
Windswept hills . . .
Yet, I
Sing of the king.

O Lord:
  Help me
  To look past the
  Dull eyes of
  Destitute souls
  And see
  Frightened children
  Fleeing
  Before the
  Avalanche of life.
  Help these leaden legs
  To run again
  The good race.
  I ask not for
  Olympic time
  But only strength
  To faithfully
  Finish
  The course.
  Help this
  Heart grown heavy
  With the sludge
  Of clogged
  Relationships
  To sing again the
  Song of Deborah.

You have told
Of ears that hear . . .
But Lord,
Who
Shall silence
The dismal
Din
Of mindless
Chatter,
And what
Shall stay
The·stride
Of
Aimless arrogance?
A ram in the thicket . . .
The bush that burns . . .
Haircoat, locust, and wild honey . . .
A star . . .
Spittle on dusty clay . . .
The tree?

THE CROSS . . .
>The single
>Brush-stroke
>Of purple
>In the
>One face
>>. . . Remembered best!
>A bruise
>That pulses
>Deep
>Within a heart
>That can
>Never   . . . Quite forget!

Today
I walked
Where
Jesus
Walked —

I had
Hoped
It would
Be
Crowded;

Indeed
I felt
His
Presence
There —

But I
Somehow
Missed
My
Friends.

Saturday:

Twelve defeated, aching hearts,
Their faith flung back with awful sting —
Death, the undefeatable death,
Had come to claim the king.

Minds shattered now by disbelief,
No longer keen with hope,
Shocked to numbness they endured — save one,
Who took the rope.

Waiting, wretched and forlorn —
Unable to conceive,
Despair filled up each soul until
It no longer could believe.

The Grief of God:

The secret sorrow —
    Quiet, constant, deep
    Always there in mask
The heart at last can weep
    For what has come — and
    In that voice the deeper sorrow,
    Suffering dumb til now,
    Is vent.
Sorrow hid in sorrow —
    Come be spent.

Catch hold —
   The hand is clean
   The eye is honest
   The smile is steady
   Catch hold!
No chance that hurt can
   Fold to crush.
And you believe . . .

Fool —
   The hand is cruel
   The eye turns hard
   The smile twists ugly
You are caught in a knot of no.

Run —
   Refuse the hand, the eye, the smile
   Answer no with no.
But then listen . . .
Thrice the cock shall crow.

Skyscraper

Strong it stood,
The cross of wood.
Strong too
The cross of steel.

The one whose shine
Is but a sign
Will rust —
It cannot feel!

Without you there . . .
I kiss the
Emptiness
Of air
And my heart
Is filled with
Sweet imaginings!

Moving memory's mist
Cloaks
The heart with the
Delicate dew
Of
Forever's longing!

Tonight . . .
I learned
That just across the room
Was
A world away!
I learned
That here
Is not there
And that
There is
Absence in presence!
Distance, dimension, and
Plane
Are discs
Easily slipped
When
There is no
Touching!
I learned to
Pile
Boxes upon boxes
And call it
Building;
I learned to
Spin
Wheels within wheels
And call it
Moving!
Tonight . . .
I learned
That just across the room
Was
A world away!

Ode to an Age

Thirty-nine
Oh, fine!
Is there choice
To voice?
To grow older
Or bolder?
          . . . certainly not colder!

Is it a shove
Into love?
Or decision
With vision?
Laughter
And after?
Bearing, sharing
          . . . most of all caring!

Tomorrow
We'll borrow
A page from an age
That's been!
To adore and explore
We'll win
          . . . life together!

Love is as
Elusive
As
A wisp of
Smoke!
Given breath
It curls
About
The sturdy logs of
Life;
Trapped and
Contained
It
Disappears
As water
Through
The fingers!

The emptiness of
Man
Can be filled
Only by
The emptiness of
The tomb.